G000168212

PLANTS
FOR THE HOME

PLANTS
FOR THE HOME

Marshall Cavendish

Edited by Susan Conder

Published by Marshall Cavendish Books Limited
58 Old Compton Street
London W1V 5PA

© Marshall Cavendish Limited 1985

Printed and bound in Italy by New Interlitho SpA
ISBN 0 86307 381 6

Half title page: *Veltheimia viridifolia, or unicorn root*
Opposite title page: *Hedera colchica, or variegated ivy*
Above: *Dracaena godseffiana, or Florida beauty*
Page 56: *Asparagus plumosus, or asparagus fern*

INTRODUCTION

Few homes today are without plants as decoration in one form or another, whether it's just simple bulbs at springtime or a complex display designed to bring year round interest to a room. However, unlike other decorations, houseplants require a fair amount of attention in order to ensure that they will remain healthy and hence make an attractive addition to the home.

Plants for the Home sets out the simple rules for houseplant success. It explains how a plant 'works' so that you can gain an insight into its requirements in the artificial environment of the home, then traces each of the steps involved in keeping and maintaining a healthy plant. From the initial stages of buying and siting right through to the more complex aspects of propagation, it covers in detail all aspects of plant maintenance. Specialities are included too – bottle gardens, bonsai and hydroponics are all discussed and fully illustrated both in colour and with step-by-step diagrams for the more difficult procedures.

In a clear concise style and fully illustrated throughout *Plants for the Home* provides all the practical information for healthy and successful growing indoors.

CONTENTS

INTRODUCTION

The wide variety of plants available today from florists, nurseries and even department stores make selection confusing to say the least. Plants with brightly coloured foliage of flowers, or with more subtle attractions such as variegated or highly sculptured leaves; plants of every possible shape and size, all presented shoulder-to-shoulder on display.

Although we have come to expect such a wide range of choice, and a tropical houseplant in a shop window seems no more unusual than bananas or pineapples at the greengrocer, this has not always been the case. For although the history of indoor plants goes back over many centuries, it is only in the last hundred years or so that the average person could take pleasure in buying and growing them.

Plants have long been collected and admired for a variety of reasons. Besides their medicinal qualities, their inherent beauty, rarity and consequent monetary value have encouraged the transporting of plants from one part of the world to another. For example, during the early part of the 17th century, at the height of tulip mania in Holland, a single bulb from Turkey was sold for the value of over ten acres of land and fortunes were made and lost dealing in tulip bulbs.

Until mid-Victorian times, the collecting of indoor plants tended to be the province of the very wealthy. The later 17th century saw collecting orange trees as the fashionable pursuit. More than 150 varieties were cultivated, but as special glass houses, or orangeries, as well as a constant supply of heat were needed to over-winter these tender subjects, it was the prerogative of the very wealthy.

By the middle of the 19th century, however, a number of social and economic changes had occurred which made collecting and displaying indoor plants more popular than it had ever been before or has been up to the present day. In England, the Industrial Revolution had, as one result, the emergence of a large and prosperous middle class, with money to spend and an inclination to spend it. Around the same period, the repeal of the glass tax, which had previously kept the use of glass in construction to a minimum, combined with the technical discoveries enabling the production of cheap glass on a large scale, resulted in the almost overnight mushrooming of private, domestic greenhouses and conservatories — no longer the province of the upper class alone, but a symbol of the widespread and newfound prosperity.

The Victorians were collectors at heart and indoor plants were no exception. The invention of the Wardian case earlier in the century had revolutionized plant collecting in far and distant countries. The case, really a glass and metal or wood airtight terrarium, allowed seeds and plants to survive the rigours of long overland travels and dangerous sea voyages to England. Before the advent of this case, most of the plants collected in tropical and subtropical regions arrived in England dead, if they arrived at all. In a storm at sea, containers full of plants were often jettisoned first and even if they remained on deck, contact with salt spray was enough to destroy the majority of them. If properly packed, the Wardian case assured a 90 per cent survival rate and the number of new tender plants arriving yearly was overwhelming. Nurseries and Botanical Gardens sent their own expeditions to the wilds of China, Japan, India, Africa and South America to discover and send back to England new plants. In addition, missionaries, the military forces and even diplomatic personnel throughout the world became sources of new material.

It was during this period that ferns reached the height of popularity. Both indoor and hardy types, from all parts of the world, were extensively collected. Most ferns thrive in the shade and the dimly lit interiors of Victorian parlours and sitting rooms suited them admirably. Hedgerows and woods were stripped as collectors searched for more and more curious specimens. The Victorians, as a whole, were intrigued by the out-of-the-ordinary, odd and bizarre, whatever the subject. Hence Venus-fly-trap plants, which trapped and consumed insects, incredibly enormous Amazonian water lilies and ferns with forked, double or otherwise distorted fronds were highly valued. Some of these newly introduced plant oddities needed very special growing conditions and the Wardian case reappeared, this time as a permanent household fixture in which difficult specimens could be grown. Large or small, highly ornate or quite plain, the Wardian case allowed plants needing a high level of humidity to co-exist in the same room as the everpresent aspidistra, or cast-iron plant, beloved by the Victorians for its ability to survive almost any growing conditions.

As fashions changed so too did the plant varieties. Although in the early 20th century indoor plants were not so popular, certain varieties came to the fore. In the 'twenties and 'thirties, for example, cacti and succulents were the favourites. However, it was in the 'forties that a now eminent English nurseryman coined the term 'houseplant' and started what has developed into something of a revolution in the world of potted plants.

In contrast to the late 19th century, there are very few new plants to be discovered in the wild today which would make first-class indoor subjects. In spite of this, new plants are constantly being put on the market. Plant breeders are now relying on a combination of scientific knowledge and skills and chance mutation to supply them with new plants, rather than sending out expensive and risky plant-hunting expeditions.

The modern, self-branching, brightly-coloured poinsettia, *Euphorbia mikkelrochford*, is a prime

The Victorians were very fond of Wardian cases such as this one. Inside a Wardian case, the atmospheric moisture and purity can be controlled; this allows for the cultivation of very tender species of ferns in an otherwise unsuitable environment. Many of the Victorian Wardian cases were quite decorative in themselves, and some were highly embellished.

example. Always a popular plant, the Christmas trade in poinsettias has been revolutionized by the use of modern growth-depressant chemicals, which ensure that the plants are the right size and in flower at the right time. A few years ago, an enormous stock plant of poinsettia arrived in England from America. It was noticed, almost accidentally, that this stock plant had the ability to produce numerous growing shoots in the axils of the lower leaves if the growing tip was removed. Normally, poinsettias produce only one new shoot where the leaf joins the stem, immediately below the pinched-out growing tip. Because of this horticultural quirk, all poinsettias propagated from this stock plant have five or six colourful flowering bracts, instead of one or two,

and a more attractive and marketable plant has resulted.

However, modern developments have not always had beneficial effects. Hardy plants, such as honeysuckle, paeony, mahonia and berberis, once recommended as houseplants, have now been eliminated as suitable subjects due to the advent of central heating. In addition, some plants which are first-class indoor subjects are slow to propagate commercially and modern nurseries tend to shy away from them. Tragically, the hardy stalwart of the Victorian era, the Aspidistra, has been foremost among the victims. It takes such a long time to produce a marketable plant that sadly it is available today only sporadically and at a high price.

9

BASIC NEEDS

For many people successful indoor growing appears largely a matter of chance. However, there is an art even a science to raising houseplants and although achieving perfection depends on a fanatic commitment to creating the correct environment, the more you know about how a plant works and its origins, the more likely you will know how to meet its needs.

Very few houseplants today originate from the world's temperate zones. As they actually evolved to succeed in the temperatures outdoors, they just do not do well in the modern, centrally-heated home. They also have a natural dormancy period in the winter months which mean that they will shed their leaves with the advent of cold weather. As houseplants are required to be displayed all year round, a plant with bare branches six months of the year is far from ideal. Ivy, and its near relative, *Fatsia*, are the main exceptions to this rule. However, they do require conditions indoors which resemble those outside as much as possible. Cool airy rooms, preferably without central heating and a spell out doors in summer are best.

Occasionally, evergreen shrubs from Mediterranean regions are attempted as indoor plants; bay, often in a clipped form, myrtle and rosemary are examples. Being evergreen, they remain attractive all year round, but the problem of excessive heat and a dry atmosphere still remains. Although Mediterranean summers are hot, dry and sunny, the winters are cool and wet and plants from this region tend to drop their leaves if confronted with unnaturally warm termperatures. The frost-free greenhouse or conservatory is much more suitable for them, or even outdoors if the site is a moderately sheltered one.

Odd as it may first seem, a large number of indoor plants are tropical or sub-tropical in origin. The

While a cool light position will suit most of these plants, because of their original environment, cryptanthus and aglaonema (front left) require warmth and Fatsia japonica (back right) prefers a cool, shady situation.

Amazon basin in South America, the Central American mainland, the Congo basin in Africa and the Indo-Malayan area of Asia have been rich sources of indoor plants. This is because the temperature and light intensity inside a house most resembles that of a tropical rain forest. The relatively constant warmth which is so harmful to plants of the temperate region is positively beneficial to the cultivation of tropical plants. Although the amount of sunlight at the tree canopy level of tropical jungles is high, very little of it reaches the forest floor. Plants growing at ground level in dense tropical forests have adapted themselves admirably to making the most of the small amount of filtered sunlight that actually penetrates the dense foliage. As a rule they are broad-leaved evergreens, with a large amount of leaf surface to make use of every bit of sunlight available. This ability serves them well in the artifical environment of a sitting room or hall where there is a very limited amount of sunlight.

Because of the continually high level of humidity present in their natural environment, leaves of tropical rain-forest plants have evolved in such a way as to be able to shed water quickly. They tend to be oval or elliptical in shape, with a smooth, shiny upper surface and an elongated end point known as a drip tip. The curious perforations in the leaves of the Swiss cheese plant are thought to be yet another method of quickly shedding excess water. While all of these qualities are functional, they make for very attractive foliage as well. Although the temperature and light intensity in an average heated room suit these plants, the atmospheric moisture which exists in a tropical rain forest is obviously lacking. The dedicated grower will try to reproduce this humidity albeit in a small way, by spraying the leaves frequently with a mist sprayer or growing the plants on a tray filled with pebbles and water so that the continual evaporation makes the air humid immediately around the plants.

At the other end of the spectrum, plants from very dry environments also make their way into shops and sitting rooms as easy-to-care-for subjects. Although it is not really possible to recreate the intensity of the sunlight in their original environment, they are able to adapt to the reduced amount of light near a relatively sunny window. Being used to long periods of drought, hot summers and cold winters, they are quite tough and will survive in a wide range of temperatures. Cacti and many other succulents originate in arid environments, where their ability to store water is essential for survival. Spines are a way of protecting the plant from browsing and grazing animals during the summer months when little else is available. *Euphorbia fulgens*, crown of thorns, is a fine example. Some euphorbias have even developed a milky sap which

can be unpleasant and is, in some cases, poisonous to animals.

The leaves on these plants, in many cases, have disappeared and the usual leaf functions are carried out by the stem. The lack of leaf surface thus reduces the transpiration rate and enables the plant to withstand the rigours of desert and semi-desert conditions.

In contrast, many South African plants, such as clivias and hippeastrums, have evolved a different method of storing food — in their bulbs. During the long hot summers of their environment, they remain dormant, but it only takes the first autumn rains to activate the production of food and the glorious flowering of these plants.

Light and shade

Plants need light to manufacture the sugars and starches which supply them with the energy to live, grow and reproduce. During this process, called

Many South African plants, such as clivias, store water in their bulbs or swollen roots for use during periods of drought.

photosynthesis, the plant uses the chlorophyll contained in the green pigment of the leaves to harness the energy in sunlight and turn carbon dioxide and water into starch and sugar. If there is insufficient light, a reduction in the amount of chlorophyll in the plant will result and the plant will be permanently weakened. It is for this reason that variegated plants tend to be weaker than their all-green counterparts; containing less chlorophyll, they manufacture less food. Likewise, they need plenty of sunlight to thrive and display their variegation fully.

Although light is necessary for a plant to live, it does not follow that the more light given, the better. The optimum amount of light needed varies enormously from plant to plant and also from season to season. It changes according to temperature and soil conditions and periods of growth and rest. Ideally, the conditions in which a plant grows in nature should be reproduced as closely as possible.

Plants respond not only to the amount of light available, but the relationship between periods of light and darkness, ie day and night. Chrysanthemums, for example, will only flower when the hours of daylight are shorter than a critical period (in this case 12 hours); many autumn-flowering species have similar requirements and are called 'short day plants'. 'Long day plants', such as evening primrose, iris and rudbeckia, will only flower if the period of light exceeds a critical amount every day. A third category, called day-neutral-plants, will flower over a wide range of light conditions.

As many indoor plants are grown for their flowers, an elementary knowledge of their light needs will result in larger and longer floral displays and a generally healthier plant.

The source of light can also have an enormous effect on the shape and attractiveness of a plant. Leaves, stems and flowers tend to grow towards a light source; this movement is called phototropism. Pot plants grown on a windowsill and not turned regularly will eventually become one-sided, each leaf facing the window in an attempt to absorb the maximum amount of light. Likewise, if the source of light is far away and weak, a plant will become drawn and spindly in its attempt to reach the light source.

Temperature

There is no one ideal temperature for all indoor plants; the optimum temperature varies enormously, depending on the natural habitat of a particular plant, its seasonal needs and even its daily needs. Perhaps the one single rule which is applicable to all indoor plants is that sudden changes of temperature should be avoided. Plants, like cold-blooded animals, tend to take on the temperature of the surrounding

environment and a sudden drop or rise can lead to wilting, leaf-drop, permanent damage and eventual death. For this reason, rooms which are heated sporadically, perhaps in the evenings, make for more difficult growing conditions than those which are kept evenly frost-free. Gas heat also presents problems; certain plants, such as begonias will simply fail to survive in the presence of gas and it is best to accept the limitation and select plants for their tolerance of gas, rather than fight a doomed battle which will sooner or later be lost.

As with light requirements, a knowledge of the original habitat is indispensable for the proper cultivation of a plant. Those from the temperate zone, for example, benefit from a gradual drop in temperature at night. This allows for a natural resting period; otherwise, all the food and energy which has been manufactured and stored during the day will be expended at night and little will be left for further growth and flowering. Tropical plants, on the other hand, resent changes in night-time temperature as conditions in their natural habitat remain relatively constant. Their period of dormancy is induced by the witholding of water during winter, while still maintaining a relatively high temperature.

Up to a certain point, the higher the temperature, the faster the rate of growth, respiration (the process by which food is broken down and energy expended) and transpiration (the process of losing water in the form of vapour from the leaf surfaces). Above a critical point, which again varies from plant to plant, all of these life processes are slowed down and the excessive heat can result in physical damage and even death.

At the other end of the scale, tolerance of cold also varies enormously. Tropical plants have a low tolerance, and even temperatures well above freezing can be fatal. Plants from the temperate zone can tolerate quite low temperatures and alpine plants, used to the rigours of a mountainous environment, lower still. It is not merely a question of tolerance, but of necessity. Periods of extreme cold allow such plants to rest and enable them to respond to the ensuing warmth of spring with renewed growth and vigour. Biennial plants will not form flowers until they have been exposed to a period of cold and seeds of many plants will not germinate unless they have been exposed to a period of very cold, even freezing, weather.

Finally, temperature should never be considered as an isolated factor. The interaction between temperature, light and water is a constantly changing one and an ideal temperature in humid conditions may be much too high for the same plant when grown in a dry atmosphere. It is really only by process of trial and error that optimum conditions are achieved.

Water

Plants, like people, are composed by volume largely of water. It is water pressure which gives a plant its rigidity and wilting is a sign that there is insufficient water present in the plant. Besides keeping a plant upright, water is used for general maintenance and growth. Although a very few plants, some orchids, for example, can get their water directly from water vapour in the air, most rely on absorbing rainwater from the soil by means of their roots.

Once water has been taken up by the roots, it is carried to the above-ground portion of the plant, where a large proportion is lost through evaporation from the leaves into the air. This process of losing water through evaporation is continual and it is when the rate of evaporation exceeds the rate at which water is taken into the roots that wilting occurs. The evaporation loss depends on many factors. The higher the temperature and light intensity, exposure to draughts and very dry atmospheric conditions all increase the rate of evaporation. Plants growing in environments where there is a high rate of water loss have developed in a way to overcome this problem. For example, plants with very waxy or hairy leaves or those with tough leathery leaves, lose less water than those with thin delicate leaves, and should be grown in a dry atmosphere.

Getting the right amount of water, both soil and atmospheric, to a plant at the correct time can be quite difficult. More indoor plants die from over-watering than any other cause and there are few hard and fast rules which are applicable to all indoor plants. *Cyperus* and *Acorus*, for example, are best grown with their roots actually submerged in water, as they are waterside plants whereas the roots of most other indoor plants would simply rot if grown in similar conditions. Again, the best guide is a thorough knowledge of a plant's original environment.

With indoor plants, it is not simply a question of the amount of water necessary, but the pattern of watering as well. Plants have adapted themselves over many years to the annual pattern of rainfall in their native habitat and this should be recreated as closely as possible in the artificial indoor environment. Desert plants, such as cacti and other succulents, are used to very long periods of drought followed by short rainy seasons and their wide-spreading shallow roots enable them to absorb as much rain as possible, even from the lightest shower. Alternatively, some desert plants have enormously long tap-roots which grow downwards until they find the water table. The succulent stems and leaves of desert plants operate in much the same way as a camel's hump, storing water and releasing it slowly over a long period. Giving such plants an even, steady supply of water is not a kindness but a certain method of killing them inadvertently.

Soils and feeding

As a growing medium, soil has a twofold purpose: it gives a plant a firm base in which to anchor itself and supplies a plant with the essential nutrients, air and water. The larger roots a plant sends into the soil tend to serve as anchoring roots, while minute root hairs do most of the absorption of water, in which are dissolved various minerals, compounds and trace elements. Unless a plant is hydrophytic, that is a plant which normally grows in water and has leaves and roots specially adapted to absorb oxygen from the surrounding water, the presence of air between and around the individual particles of soil is of primary importance. In a good, free-draining potting compost there are many tiny pockets of air; in water-logged soil, these spaces are filled with water. As a result, the roots cannot breathe and the plant drowns. In addition, the lack of air also kills the beneficial bacteria and a sour, acid soil results.

Water and soil are further interrelated by the fact that not all the water in the soil is available to a plant. Soil holds water in tension, and the lower the water content the greater the tension with which the water is held. This means that the roots will have little trouble in absorbing water from a throughly damp compost, but the drier it becomes, the harder it is to extract the remaining water.

When a plant grows in its natural environment, the nutrients it removes from the soil are constantly being replaced in the form of dead vegetable and animal matter which decay and are returned to the soil. In the forest, the fallen leaves and debris establish a balance between nutrients taken away and nutrients returned. The opposite is true for pot plants. They are required to live, and indeed thrive, in a very small quantity of soil from which all nutrients are removed and none returned naturally. For this reason, the initial composition of the growing medium is of the utmost importance, as even the most minor imbalance can prove fatal. Coupled with this is the need to replace nutrients artificially in exactly the right quantity so that the plant does not starve or grow too weak and lush through overfeeding.

Garden soil, however good for outdoor plants, is not suitable for use with indoor plants. It is highly unlikely that the texture and chemical composition would come up to the rigorous standards required for an indoor growing medium. Moreover, a garden soil contains innumerable weed seeds, as well as bacteria and other soil organisms which may be relatively

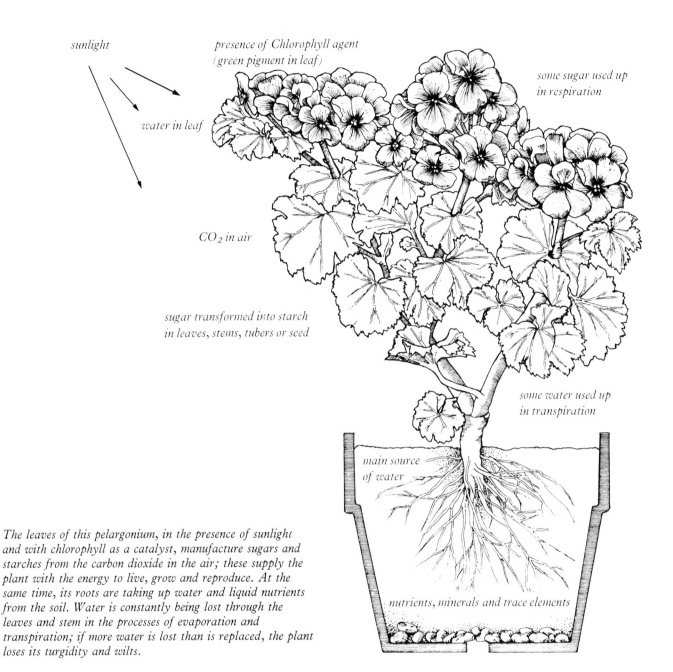

sunlight

presence of Chlorophyll agent
(green pigment in leaf)

some sugar used up
in respiration

water in leaf

CO_2 in air

sugar transformed into starch
in leaves, stems, tubers or seed

some water used up
in transpiration

main source
of water

nutrients, minerals and trace elements

*The leaves of this pelargonium, in the presence of sunlight
and with chlorophyll as a catalyst, manufacture sugars and
starches from the carbon dioxide in the air; these supply the
plant with the energy to live, grow and reproduce. At the
same time, its roots are taking up water and liquid nutrients
from the soil. Water is constantly being lost through the
leaves and stem in the processes of evaporation and
transpiration; if more water is lost than is replaced, the plant
loses its turgidity and wilts.*

harmless outdoors but which will thrive and cause
absolute havoc indoors. A good, open loamy soil can,
however, be used as the base of a potting compost
if it is partially sterilized by steaming it for twenty
minutes at a temperature of 93°C (200°F). This is hot
enough to kill weed seeds and harmful bacteria, but
leaves the beneficial bacteria unharmed. Special soil
sterilizing units are available commercially, but it is
not really worth the expense unless large quantities
of soil are involved. The sterilized loam is then mixed
with peat or leafmould and fertilizers according to
one of several formulae.

Standardized ready-mixed composts for indoor

plants are well worth the initial expense as all the
guesswork has been removed and they are virtually
risk-free. John Innes composts are available in three
recipes, each suitable for a particular type of plant.

John Innes no. 1 is best for slow-growing plants,
newly-rooted cuttings and cacti and succulents as it
contains a relatively low amount of nutrients. John
Innes no. 2 contains twice as much fertilizer and is
probably the best all-purpose compost, while John
Innes no. 3 is good for quick-growing plants, as it
contains the greatest concentration of fertilizer.
These three formulae, with occasional modifications,
should meet the needs of most indoor plants.

LIVING WITH PLANTS

Although there are no rules guaranteeing house-plant success, there are general guidelines starting with initial selection which, if followed, can ensure a healthy and attractive display of indoor plants.

The eventual purchaser may feel that the plant's past life in the nursery is no concern of his. However, the skillful rearing of a plant before it reaches the display counter is the first factor which determines whether or not the plant will do well once purchased. Feeble plants which have been badly raised will almost invariably remain feeble. If you know a reputable grower, he is the man from whom to buy your plants. Even if the plants are slightly more expensive, it will be well worth it in the long run.

If, on the other hand, you do not have the good fortune of knowing such a grower, the next best thing is to get your plants from a reliable and under-standing retailer. Many a plant has left the grower in the peak of health, only to pine away in some draughty corner or perched on a high, inaccessible shelf in a store, getting little or no water.

The sort of plant to look for is one that is crisp, fresh and with an obvious air of good health about it. Avoid plants which have a battered appearance or equally battered wrappings around them, ostensibly to protect the plant. This paper frequently conceals

When buying poinsettias, closely inspect the tiny flower buds in the centre of the bracts; select a plant with these buds still closed to ensure a long period of floral display.

defects lower down the stem of the plant in question. The efficient grower would never dream of sending out delicate plants without the protective covering of a paper sleeve, but the plants must never remain in these covers for a moment longer than is necessary. The sensible retailer removes these covers as soon as the plants arrive so the plants get plenty of fresh air and the customers can clearly see what they are purchasing.

When selecting a plant try to avoid those with slimy pots, dirty labels or no labels at all, brown or yellow leaves or disfigured growth. Care and cultivation tags attached to the plant are seldom very explicit, largely because of their size, but they do give some guidance about the needs of a particular plant. They will usually indicate what sort of light and temperature conditions the plant needs and also its water requirements.

Although the timing is not as critical with foliage plants, it is most important to buy flowering plants at the right stage of development. Azaleas, for example, should not be bought if their flowers are all fully open or if the flower buds are too tightly shut. An azalea in full bloom will very quickly be past its best; buds which are too tightly closed may never open satisfactorily. The best plants are those which have a reasonable number of flowers fully open and plenty of buds showing colour. Chrysanthemums, on the other hand, should be bought with flowers well open or the buds may turn black and be a total disappointment.

Although the attractive red part of a poinsettia is not a flower but bracts, or coloured leaves, they do have insignificant flowers in the centres of the bracts and these are a good guide to the health and quality of the plant. The flowers should be in the bud stage or with the stamens showing through. If the flowers have fallen off it is an indication that the plant has had its coloured bracts for much too long and will quickly lose its attractiveness.

In cold weather, it is most important to avoid buying African violets with leaves which are curled under at the edges, as this is a sign that the plant has been exposed to damaging cold conditions. Also avoid plants with wet, decaying flowers, as these will drop into the central rosette of leaves and encourage further rot.

When choosing cyclamen, look for a well-flowered plant but avoid plants with flowers which have brown edges on the petals; this indicates that flowering is nearly over. However, if an otherwise healthy plant has one or two such flowers amongst plenty of flower buds it is still worth buying because older flowers die naturally as the newer ones are formed. Once a flower has died, remove it, together with its stalk, to keep

The amount of light available is perhaps the most important factor in siting a plant indoors; this shrimp plant needs plenty of light, but some shade during the hot summer months.

the plant looking attractive and also to discourage rot. A final word of advice about cyclamen: it is not necessarily the biggest plant which is the best value. Those with considerable top growth compared to the pot size will probably have used up all the nutrients in the soil and once they are removed from the ideal growing conditions of a commercial greenhouse they often rapidly succumb to the more testing environment indoors. It is much better to select well-budded plants that are in proportion to the containers in which they are grown.

Initial siting and design

Unlike a piece of ornamental china, which is displayed entirely as a matter of personal taste, there is a certain amount of objectivity and cold science involved in siting indoor plants. A plant will show its dislike for an unsuitable position by dying, although this is usually a gradual process and reassessment at the first sign of discontent will almost certainly remedy the situation.

The amount of light available to a plant is perhaps

the most important factor; the light can be either natural sunlight or artificial light. Plants thriving in full sun should be sited as close as possible to a sunny, south or west facing window. Keep in mind, however, that light is not the only consideration. Many windows have radiators directly beneath them and the rising heat can present a real problem. Additionally, unless windows are double glazed, winter frost can penetrate the glass and physically damage tender subjects. Also solar gain during the hottest summer weather can make a window-sill much too hot for comfort. Often, the best position for a plant changes from season to season, as the plant's needs and local conditions change. Plants close to a window during winter when the amount of light is low, for example, may do best moved slightly away from the glass during the hottest and brightest summer weather. Some indoor plants, however, enjoy a brief spell outdoors during summer, in a sheltered position. Aspidistras and citrus bushes are examples. Aspidistras prefer semi-shade and full sun will ripen the wood of citrus bushes, resulting in heavier flowering the following year.

Artificial light can be used to augment a low level of natural sunlight, but this can be expensive in terms of electricity costs. Special fluorescent lights, particularly suitable for indoor plant-growing, are available and warm white tubes are also good. However, be careful not to put the artificial light source too close to the plants, as it gives off a lot of direct heat which can scorch the leaves. Some plants, such as African violet, actually do better when grown under artificial light. For such plants you can make or buy special plant-growing cases, complete with heating tubes at the bottom of the case and fluorescent lights suspended above. These cases protect plants from draughts and are economical in terms of heating. The amount of reflected light in a room can be increased by using a very pale or white paint on the walls; in this way dimly lit basement rooms can be made to seem sunnier and more attractive to both people and plants.

Direct sources of heat should be avoided, such as cookers, storage heaters, electric fires, fireplaces and even refrigerators. Draughts are equally devastating, as they increase the rate of transpiration and a plant can quickly become dessicated. For this reason, keep plants well away from air conditioning vents and badly fitted windows and doors. Draught-proof stripping fitted to windows can minimize the problem and make the room more comfortable for all concerned.

The various rooms of a house tend to have different growing conditions, each suitable for a particular type of plant. Bathrooms, for example, have a relatively high degree of humidity coupled with low levels of direct sunlight — ideal growing conditions for ferns. Kitchens may have more light but tend to have fluctuating temperatures caused by cooking, bedrooms are generally kept cooler than the sitting room and kitchen and are perfect for temperate plants, such as ivies.

Once the hazards of siting indoor plants have been identified and overcome, plants can be considered as design elements. On a functional level, plants can be used to conceal unattractive aspects of a room such as pipes or bad plasterwork. Large free-standing plants or climbers trained up trelliswork can be used as room dividers, giving privacy and a feeling of enclosure at a smaller cost than building a wall would entail.

Groups of plants can act as focal points, in much the same way as a piece of sculpture. Apart from the design aspect, plants growing together tend to benefit from the association. Watering and general maintenance will automatically become easier, and the atmosphere immediately around the plants will be relatively moist and beneficial to the plants' general health and growth. Delicate foliage can serve as a contrast to the somewhat harsh appearance of very modern furniture or humanize and soften a bare, cold-looking office space. For many people, plants give a feeling of peace and restfulness; because plants are living, they are constantly changing and developing and this process is a fascinating one to observe, over a period of weeks, months or even years. Their predictable periods of growth and flowering, followed by periods of dormancy, offer a sense of stability and contact with nature that is so often lacking in much of modern life.

Implements

For indoor growing, the most essential piece of equipment is a container. Until relatively recently, these were made of clay or earthenware. Nowadays, plastic containers have become increasingly popular and in some places it is difficult to buy a new clay pot. Both clay and plastic pots have their supporters and it is really a matter of personal preference, as it is generally accepted that plants can be equally well grown in either type. Clay pots are porous and let air and moisture through in both directions. This allows the soil inside the pot to breathe but also allows the water inside the pot to evaporate very quickly. The clay itself absorbs a great deal of water and for this reason plants grown in clay pots will need heavier

Groups of plants, attractively displayed, can act as focal points in much the same way as a piece of sculpture; here philodendron and two varieties of tradescantia are combined.

and more frequent watering than those in plastic pots.

Clay pots are heavier and relatively bulky compared to plastic ones; commercial growers, because they deal in great numbers of pots, tend to choose plastic. In addition, clay pots are more expensive, more easily broken and the labour costs involved in cleaning and sterilizing them for re-use prohibitive. Commercial considerations, however, are not necessarily relevant to home growers. Many people feel that the more natural, organic appearance of clay pots complement the foliage and flowers of a plant and do not mind the extra watering.

Clay pots should be thoroughly soaked, preferably overnight, before using to wash away any salts left from firing and also to keep the clay from absorbing excessive amounts of water from the compost. Because plastic pots are non-porous, the soil inside them tends to heat up and they should never be sited in direct sunlight for this reason.

Both clay and plastic pots are available in a variety of sizes, all measured according to the diameter at the rim. In former times, 2.5cm (1in) pots were available but these are really too small to be practical for most indoor needs, and 6.2cm (2in) is the smallest useful pot generally available. Sizes range up to 25cm (10in) and 30cm (12in) pots. Half-pots are shallow pots, half the depth of normal pots with the same diameter. These are particularly useful for shallow-rooted plants such as alpines. For visual and horticultural reasons, plants should never be put in excessively large pots. Besides looking out-of-balance, the areas of soil which are not in contact with the plant's roots may turn sour and some plants actually flower better if they are in containers slightly too small for their root ball.

The holes in the bottom of clay and plastic pots allow excess water to drain away and are essential for the well-being of the plant. Ornamental glazed pottery, bamboo or reed outer pots can be used to conceal the plastic or clay pot. Besides their attractive appearance, these cache-pots can also be functional; by filling the space between the inner and outer pot with moist peat or moss, a humid atmosphere can be created immediately around the plant.

There are a few basic tools which make indoor growing easier although they are not strictly necessary. Foremost among these is a long-spouted watering can. Unlike outdoor gardening, where water going astray does little harm, expensive carpeting and wallpaper can be damaged by unnecessary drenching, and a long-spouted watering can allows for a

Climbing plants with aerial roots, such as this philodendron, look best when given some form of substantial support.

measure of control. A sharp knife and secateurs make cutting and pruning easier and a spray gun is useful to clean and mist leaves. Those plants with hairy or furry leaves should not be exposed to water and can be cleaned with a soft-bristled brush, cotton wool, or a soft cloth. Bamboo canes are useful for supporting climbing plants together with twine or special metal rings for attaching the plant to the pole.

Many plants, particularly those with aerial roots, such as *Monstera deliciosa*, grow best when given a vertical, mossy support on which to cling. These supports can be quite expensive to buy but they are not at all difficult to make as long as you can obtain the right materials. Basically, the support has to be strong enough to bear the weight of the plant and, at the same time, not look overbearing or unsightly. It also has to be strong enough to last the life of the plant as the aerial roots take a very firm hold and the moss and stake virtually become part of the plant. Wooden supports are not advisable as they tend to rot at the base part-way through the plant's life, causing all sorts of problems. Lightweight, rigid plastic tubing is a better material, provided it can be entirely concealed by the sphagnum moss.

When measuring for the support, allow for at least 60cm (2ft) more than the height of the plant. If necessary, you can extend the height of the tubing support by inserting an additional tube, with a smaller diameter, into the top of the first one. You will need good quality sphagnum moss, not too thin in consistency. Clear nylon fishing line is ideal for binding the moss to the support, as it is very strong and does not rot. When fixing the moss to the support, remember to leave the bottom of the support free of moss, so it can be inserted into the soil. Spray the moss regularly, to keep it moist and encourage the plant's roots to cling to the support.

Watering

Watering is potentially the most lethal routine in plant maintenance and the one most likely to go wrong for the enthusiastic beginner. Giving just a drop more water is the normal response whenever a plant looks unhappy and if a plant looks in the prime of health it is often tempting to 'reward' it with an extra drink. Such thinking can be, and all too often is, fatal.

As a general rule, there are four major periods when plants need more water — in the growing season; in warm conditions; in a dry atmosphere and when in bud and flower. Many plants, however, begin their annual growth below the surface of the compost; once the roots have begun growing, leaf-growth above ground will become evident. Ideally, you should commence more frequent watering when

the roots begin to grow, but unfortunately, there is nothing visible at this time. Generally, by mid-spring most plants have begun new growth; alternatively, you can very gently tap the root ball out of the pot and look for the presence of white roots, which are young ones. Towards the end of summer, watering should gradually be decreased, as it is not a good idea to encourage the plant to put out new growth which will not have a chance to harden off.

It is often difficult to assess how frequently a plant needs watering. In general, if a pot is filled with roots there is less compost to retain water and the mass of roots will absorb it quickly. Newly potted plants will need less frequent watering than well established, even pot-bound specimens. Additionally, if a potting compost is based on peat, it will dry out much more quickly than one based on heavy loam, and will consequently need more frequent watering.

Unfortunately, the symptoms displayed for insufficient water are similar to those for excessive water. Plants which are literally drowning will have yellowed leaves which wilt and eventually fall and will most probably drop the flower buds before they open. Unfortunately, plants which are dying of thirst react the same way, and a certain amount of common sense is called for.

There are tell-tale signs about the moisture content of the soil. Clay pots, when tapped, will produce a ringing, high sound if the soil is dry and a dull thudding sound if the soil is moist. Be careful, however, as pots which are cracked will make a dull thudding sound regardless of the soil's moisture content. It is more difficult to tell with plastic pots or those containing a peat-based compost. The weight of the pot, plant and compost, when lifted, is the best indication; it will feel very light if the compost is dry. You can, after a little experience, judge fairly accurately the moisture content of the compost by pressing down on the surface with your thumb and finger; alternatively, you can purchase a soil moisture indicator.

If, after a reasonable assessment, you decide a plant needs water, then go about it in the proper way. Giving small amounts of water which slightly moisten the surface of the compost but do little else is pointless. Thorough waterings, with periods between to allow the soil to dry out slightly, are best. If the compost is so dry that it has shrunk from the sides of the pot, submerge the pot in a basin or bucket of water and leave it until air bubbles have stopped

If the compost has dried out, submerge the pot in a bucket of water until air bubbles disappear (1). Cyclamen can be watered from below to avoid wetting the corm (2). An outer container filled with moist peat creates a damp atmosphere (3).

rising from the surface of the water. If the compost is not bone-dry, however, do not give so much water that a heavy amount collects in the plate or saucer in which the pot is standing, as many of the nutrients contained in the compost will be washed out with the water. In any case, plants should never be left standing in dishes of water (unless they are waterside plants), as root rot will quickly set in. Peat-based composts will need more frequent checking than loam-based ones, as they tend to dry out much more quickly and, once dry, are hard to saturate thoroughly. As a rule, watering should be done in the morning. This is because the temperature is rising and the plant's need for water is greater. Also, plants left too damp over night are very vulnerable to fungal infections.

Some plants quite definitely resent water on their leaves and flowers: gloxinias and African violets, with their woolly, velvety leaves are two prime examples. Water collecting on the top of the cyclamen corm will cause rot to set in and some people advocate watering it from below. A traditional method of watering cyclamens is to place the pot on a small block of wood, 2.5cm (1in) thick in a water-tight bowl. Pour enough water in the bowl to come 2.5cm (1in) above the bottom of the flowerpot. The water will be absorbed by the roots of the cyclamen, while the corm remains dry. For African violets and gloxinias, a long-necked watering can will give some measure of control and you should be able to avoid getting water on the leaves.

For plants which enjoy a humid atmosphere, it is impractical to turn the whole of your living room into a steaming tropical jungle. Microclimates of moist atmosphere can be created by plunging the pot in question into a larger container which is packed with moist peat. Alternatively, stand the pot, or group of pots, in a large trough or tray filled with moist pebbles or gravel; the water will gently evaporate into the air immediately surrounding the plant.

Feeding

As with watering, feeding is largely a matter of striking a happy medium between starving a plant of nutrients and gorging it. Enthusiastic generosity in the matter of feeding is no substitute for common sense combined with a knowledge of the right time to feed. As a general rule, dormant plants should not be given fertilizers, nor should cuttings or

If you are unable to water a plant while on holiday, there are several ways to meet its water needs for short periods of time: strips of absorbent cloth with one end tucked firmly in the soil and the other in a pan of water (1), an air-tight, transparent plastic bag (2) or water diffuser (3).

seedlings without fully formed roots. Plants which have been left to dry out inadvertantly should be given plenty of water to revive them before any fertilizers are given, as dessicated plants can be harmed by taking up nutrients.

Nutrients are needed during a plant's growing season, particularly when it is about to flower and when it is in flower. Tell-tale signs of growth are the appearance of young shoots and leaves. Should an immature plant fail to grow in the normal growing season, or should it produce unnaturally yellow leaves, this may be due to a lack of food. Be careful, however, as yellow leaves can also be symptomatic of insufficient or excessive water, or too little or too much light and it is really a process of elimination to discover the cause.

There are basically two types of plant food: organic and inorganic. The former are those chemical compounds containing carbon and are usually derived from living organisms. Manure, spent hops, garden compost and seaweed are bulky organic manures, while dried blood, hoof and horn and bone meal are non-bulky organic fertilizers. Inorganic fertilizers are those not containing carbon; artificially manufactured, the nutrients are immediately available to the plant. Basic slag, sulphate of potash and sulphate of ammonia are examples.

Whether a fertilizer is organic or inorganic, plants can only absorb the nutrients contained in them in liquid form. Bulky organic manures generally take longer for the nutrients to break down to a form readily available to plants, and this process of decomposing is aided by the various micro-organisms found in soil. While eminently suitable for outdoor gardening, where their bulky substance will do much to improve the texture of the soil, there are certain drawbacks to using organic manures indoors. Besides the odour, they often harbour pests, diseases and weed seeds and they are not really suitable for the small-scale activity of growing potted indoor plants.

Inorganic fertilizers are much more practical for indoor growing. Although they do little to improve the texture of the compost, proprietary potting composts, whether soil-based or peat-based, are already of the right consistency and do not need the bulk provided by organic manures. Many are available in concentrated liquid form and must be diluted before use. Always follow manufacturer's instructions, as excessive amounts of nutrients can be very damaging to the plant. They are also available as soluble powder and pellets, and again, manufacturer's instructions must be strictly followed. Inorganic fertilizers contain the proper amounts of

Platycerium bifurcatum, or stag's horn fern, is epiphytic; using tree branches for support it feeds from nutrients dissolved in rainwater in its cup-shaped frond base.

the three basic elements necessary for a plant to survive: nitrates for growth and rich green leaf colour, potash for the encouragement of flowers and fruit, as well as for keeping the growth from becoming too lush and soft, and phosphates for a healthy stem and root system. As peat-based composts have virtually no inherent fertilizers, plants growing in this medium will need more frequent feeding than those grown in soil-based, John Innes compounds, which already contain a certain amount of slow-acting nutrients. Besides watering nutrients into the soil, they can also be sprayed directly onto the leaves; such foliar sprays are often used as quick stimulants for ailing plants.

Repotting

Potting up, potting on and repotting are all similar processes. However, they all occur at different stages of a plant's development. First comes potting up. This is the initial transfer of newly rooted seedlings or cuttings from the seed or cutting compost, which has no nutritional value, into individual pots containing slightly richer compost. Seedlings tend to come up quite thickly in the seed pan and cuttings are usually placed close together until they root. Once germination and rooting have occurred, the young plants need less crowded conditions so by potting them up individually, each plant has a chance to develop a good root system.

When the seedlings are large enough to handle or the cuttings are well-rooted, begin potting them up. A useful tool to have for this operation is a pair of long and finely tipped tweezers. Normally the tweezers are held in the left hand so that their prongs, gently grip the stem of the seedling beneath the bottom set of leaves. During the lifting and transferring, hold the seedling in place very gently by one of the leaves. Before placing the young plant into its new pot, make a depression in the compost large enought to accommodate the roots. Use your index finger or the end of a pencil to make the depression. You need then only gently cover the roots with potting compost pushed in from around each depression, using the fingers or the flat end of a tongue depressor. Make sure the roots of the seedlings are covered and that they are planted deep enough. The initial pot into which the seedling or rooted cutting is placed should be quite small, 7.5cm (3in) is by far large enough; if the pots are too big the soil will turn sour and no advantage will be gained by the plant. For several days after potting up, shade the plants from direct sunlight until they resume growth and make sure they are well watered.

Potting on is the next stage and is normally carried out when a plant has outgrown its container. There

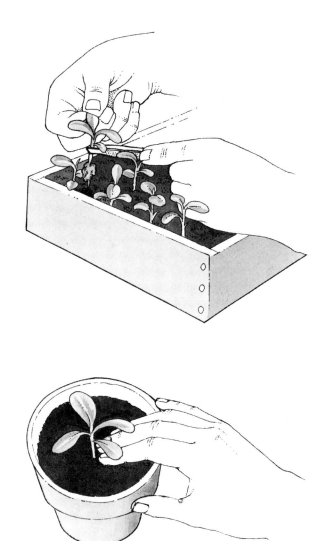

Once seedlings have germinated in a seed box or pan, the resulting seedlings tend to be overcrowded and can quickly become drawn and spindly from too much competition. As soon as they are large enough to handle, pot them up individually into small pots, firming the compost with your fingers.

are several signs which indicate that an immature plant is ready for potting on; it may have stopped growing, or roots may be appearing out of the bottom of the drainage hole at the base of the container. The secret of success with potting on is to increase the size of the pot only slightly each time; as a general rule, there should be no more than 2.5cm (1in) of space between the root ball of the plant and the sides of the new pot. This empty space is filled with fresh compost into which the roots will quickly grow. Most potting on is done in late winter or early spring, while the plant is still dormant, to avoid shocking the plant.

Roots growing out of the drainage hole are a good indication that the plant has become pot-bound and needs potting on (1). Using a slightly larger pot which is scrupulously clean and contains fresh compost, transplant gently and carefully (2). Potting on completed: note the space left at the top of the pot for water and the bottom layer of drainage material (3).

Make sure the pots into which the plants are transferred are scrupulously clean. If there are particles of soil clinging to the side, roots will become entangled in them and when the time comes to repot the plant, it will be practically impossible to remove the plant without damaging the roots.

Put a layer of drainage material at the bottom of the pot. It is essential that the plant will be at the same level in its new pot as it was in its previous one and, if need be, put a layer of fresh compost above the drainage material to bring the level up. Whenever potting, use moist but not too wet compost. If it is saturated and dripping water it will be difficult to compact properly and may congeal into a solid, airless mass of soil.

Holding your fingers round the base of the stem with the palm of your hand covering the soil, invert the pot and give it a sharp tap on the base. The plant, with its root ball intact, should slip easily from the pot. If it does not, after several repeated attempts, you may have to sacrifice the container. Carefully slit the side of plastic pots with a sharp secateur and remove the plant. If the pot is clay, then gently crack it with a hammer; be careful, however, as excessive enthusiasm when cracking open clay pots may lead to damage to the root ball.

Once the plant is free of its container, inspect the bottom of the root ball and carefully remove any pieces of crocks which may have become entangled in the roots. Then lower the plant into its new pot and, holding it with one hand, carefully work the new soil round the roots with the other. After the sides have been filled, give the pot a sharp rap on a table surface to help the plant and compost to settle. If the compost is peat based, compress it down with your fingers as well; alternatively, use a wood soil dibber with a rounded bottom. Make sure the final level of the soil is about 2.5cm (1in) below the rim of the pot, to allow for ease of watering. As with potting up, the plants should receive shelter from strong sunlight and slightly more water than normal until they have recovered from potting on.

Repotting refers to the process of transferring a mature plant which has completely filled its container with roots into another pot of the same size. This is usually done while the plant is dormant. The advantage gained from such a manoeuvre is that old, worn-out compost is replaced with fresh compost. It sometimes involves reducing the size of the rootball to encourage the production of fresh roots. Bonsai plants are regularly repotted to keep them healthy, but it is not a process to be embarked on lightly. If a plant has reached full size and appears not to thrive, it may be due to lack of nutrients, which can be remedied by giving a dilute liquid feed

or a top dressing of fresh compost. Alternatively, try changing its position in relation to the amount of light or warmth it receives; leave repotting as a last resort.

A healthy and well-maintained group planting: the vertical dieffenbachia is set off by the trailing stems of the delicate Ficus pumila and the golden variegated Scindapsus aureus.

General maintenance

Besides watering, feeding and potting on, there are numerous small tasks which, if conscientiously carried out, make all the difference between a meagre plant and a flourishing one. Little and often might be the best guide; do not treat your plants like cupboards, to be spring-cleaned once a year and ignored for the next twelve months. If you see a dead or diseased leaf, remove it immediately. Besides improving the general appearance of the plant, it will discourage the various pests and diseases which thrive on dead plant tissue. The same goes for yellow leaves; once a leaf which is normally green turns yellow it will not recover and should be removed and consigned to the dustbin. Do not confuse yellowed leaves with the slight lack of colouring which occurs when plants are in need of feeding; the leaves which are removed should be bright yellow or else withered and lifeless.

Climbing plants that produce untidy growth should have their stems tied (not too tightly) to a

29

suitable support. Some climbing plants, such as ivy, tend to lose most of their lower leaves and produce young growth only at the top of the stems; these will be vastly improved in appearance if some of the longer growth is trained downwards to fill in the gaps at the base.

Plants with large, naturally glossy leaves should be dusted now and again to keep the leaves shiny. Although all sorts of chemical concoctions can be purchased to spray on the leaves for a glossy appearance, they can be positively harmful to some plants and should never be used on the soft young growth

Vigorous climbing plants such as bougainvillea can get out of hand if growth is not controlled. Stems can be trained up bamboo or plastic poles or in a circle around wire.

at the top of a plant. A quick wipe with a soft duster will suffice most of the time. Occasionally use a moistened soft cloth or sponge to do a thorough job.

To counteract the effects of a dry atmosphere, periodically spray the leaves of plants with tepid water. Not all plants appreciate a humid atmosphere, however; saintpaulias and other downy-leaved plants should not be sprayed. As a rule, plants exposed to full sunlight should not be sprayed as the droplets of water on the leaves can cause scorch.

Perhaps the most controversial of all aspects of plant care, is that of plant psychology. Although the commercial grower of indoor plants may be a trifle cynical about the idea of plants as responsive, sensitive creatures, when he is surrounded by literally millions of them during the course of his working life, the householder can, and frequently does, adopt an entirely different attitude. For many people, plants grown indoors take on a completely different meaning from those in the vegetable garden and even decorative outdoor plants. They are often looked upon as friends and it is not unusual to find a favourite monstera named Fred, or a rubber plant named George, and so on. Plants received as gifts are sometimes named after the donor, thus forming a living link between the two people involved and should anything unfortunate happen to the plant, the feelings of guilt become even stronger because of what the plant symbolized.

Talking and even singing to plants in order to get positive responses from them, by way of bigger and better leaves and flowers, has long been practised. This seems to get results in two ways. Obviously, if one stops to have a word with the Swiss cheese plant when passing, one is more likely to notice any defects, such as excessive dryness at the roots or the presence of pests.

Secondly, recent experiments have shown that plants actually do respond positively to such human pleasures as the presence of classical music. Likewise, electrodes from lie-detectors attached to plants and used to measure their responses to various situations have indicated that plants do experience rudimentary pain and fear when harmed or threatened with harm. These same tests, which were carried out by an American lie detector expert, indicated that plants have the ability to remember specific incidents and would react negatively when someone who had previously harmed them reappeared.

Although these conclusions do not automatically commit one to thinking of plants as quasi-human, they do widen the scope of interaction between plants and people. They also suggest the possibility that the proverbial green fingers is not so much a matter of luck as empathy to which plants happily respond.

30

Propagation

When raising new plants from seed, cuttings, division or air layering, a few simple rules will ensure a high rate of success. Perhaps the most important is cleanliness. Everything associated with the operation must be spotlessly clean; previously used pots and boxes must be thoroughly scrubbed and the propagation mixture must be sterile (not a handful of soil from the garden).

To produce roots of their own, all cuttings of indoor plants will require a minimum temperature

Impatiens, or busy lizzy, benefits from periodical pinching out of growing tips to keep the plant from getting leggy.

of around 18°C (65°F); slightly higher temperatures are, on the whole, beneficial, but very hot and dry conditions can be calamitous. There are many small propagating cases available at a reasonable cost and these are ideal for small cuttings. More expensive propagating cases are available, with a built-in heating element, but there is no need to go to the extra expense if the propagator can be placed over

Busy lizzies are among the easiest plants to propagate, simply place cuttings in a bottle of water to root.

Spider plants produce large quantities of plantlets which can be potted up individually and detached from the mother.

a radiator that is operating constantly, day and night. Keeping an even, steady temperature is important, as few cuttings will do well in fluctuating temperatures.

Given proper cleanliness and temperature, the most important factor is the propagating material itself. Scrappy odds and ends taken from tired and sickly plants will almost inevitably fail. Select firm and healthy material for propagation or the whole exercise will be a waste of time.

Perhaps the best standard cutting compost is one composed of equal parts, by volume, of fresh peat and sharp sand. The sand must be sharp and the peat sphagnum and not sedge, as the latter holds too much water and is less free draining; Vermiculite is another good cutting compost. Whatever the compost, it should be moist enough for a little water to show between your fingers when a handful is compressed.

All this having been said, there is many a healthy houseplant which started life on its own in nothing more than a bottle filled with water with a piece of kitchen foil pressed over the top — the stem of the cutting is pushed through a hole in the middle of the foil so the stem reaches water and the leaf rests on the foil. Warmth and light are still necessary, but indirect light is best; any cutting exposed to full sunlight will simply shrivel up. Some good plants to propagate by this elementary bottle of water and foil method are African violets, ivies, busy lizzies and spider plants. Success is almost inevitable with these plants and, having been encouraged, more difficult subjects may then be attempted.

Plants which produce tiny, complete plantlets on the ends of runners, or stolons, are the easiest of all to propagate. Besides the spider plant (*Chlorophytum comosum*), mother-of-thousands (*Saxifraga sarmentosa*) is another good subject. Pegged down in any reasonable growing mixture, these young plantlets will quickly produce roots of their own while still attached by the stolon to the parent plant. Once well-rooted, they can be severed from the parent plant and potted up to grow on independently. Unlike most other cuttings, a peat and sand mixture is not usually suitable, as the young plants quickly become starved of nourishment and lose their colour.

Another simple yet successful method of propagation is the division of a large plant, complete with roots, into several new individuals. Aspidistras are suitable subjects for division, but there are many others. Before beginning, water the plant thoroughly; once moist, remove the plant and carefully shake off as much of the potting mixture as possible. Then gently tease apart the roots to provide several independent plants. Older clumps, however, will require more than teasing apart; it may be necessary to use a knife to divide the tough rhizomes, or even a sharp spade. Whatever the method of division, the new plants should be potted up as soon as possible into a rich growing mixture. Peat and sand is inadvisable, as these plants already have functioning roots and will need a growing medium which can provide nutrients.

Its long, arching stolons bearing perfectly formed plants at the tips make chlorophytum an attractive subject.

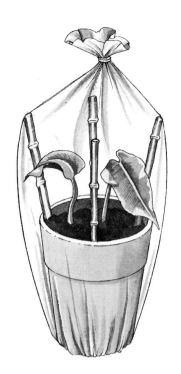

Aspidistras, or cast iron plants, can be propagated by division in spring; carefully prise apart the roots.

To keep new cuttings from wilting until roots have formed, enclose them in an air-tight, transparent polythene bag.

Cuttings are slightly more difficult because when they are removed from the parent plant they continue to lose water through the leaves, or transpire and, as they have no roots with which moisture can be replaced, they will quickly die. Most commercial growers, and many keen amateurs, have overcome this problem with a piece of equipment called a mist unit. This apparatus contains a series of fine jets of water which are activated either according to a set time clock or by an electronic 'leaf' which measures the amount of moisture over the bed of cuttings. The mist unit ensures that the surfaces of the cuttings never dry out and a greater success rate ensues.

Mist units are expensive, however, and there are other methods of overcoming this problem which are suitable for the amateur dealing with a small number of plants. Many of the easier plants, such as ivies, do perfectly well if the cuttings are put in small pots which are then covered with a thin sheet of polythene. The polythene will considerably reduce transpiration and the cuttings should root within two or three weeks. Remove the polythene periodically to reduce the risk of rot setting in; as soon as the cuttings show signs of growth the polythene should be removed completely. Alternatively, cuttings placed in small pots can be protected by enclosing them in airtight polythene bags which are supported by one or two canes to prevent the bags from collapsing onto the cuttings.

The advent of hormone rooting powders and liquids has made propagation very much easier and the success rate higher. With hormone liquids, the cutting is removed from the parent plant and dipped in the liquid rooting stimulant before being inserted in the rooting medium. With powder, cuttings should be dipped in water first, so the powder will adhere more readily.

It is a good idea to make a hole in the rooting compost to the depth that the cutting is likely to reach. It should not be too deep, as the end of the cutting should rest on the rooting mixture at the bottom of the hole. If the hole is too deep, the cuttings will swing in mid-air and be unable to root satisfactorily. Once the cuttings are in position, give a final watering, using a fine rose, before covering the cuttings with polythene or the lid of the propagating case.

Although much is written about the best time of the year to take cuttings, the vast majority of foliage plant cuttings will root at almost any time of year, given proper heat and moisture. In less than perfect conditions, however, late spring and early summer are best. The plant, once it has rooted, then has a whole growing season before it and its chances of survival are quite high.

Ficus robusta, the rubber plant, is one of the most popular indoor plants and has a definite time of year when cuttings should be taken. In the winter months the plant is dormant and less sap is likely to be lost in the process of taking cuttings. The top section of the plant, with three leaves attached, will produce a very respectable-looking plant in a relatively short time, while cuttings taken with a single leaf and piece of stem from lower down the plant will be rather sparse and awkward looking for quite some time. To take the cuttings, use a sharp knife or secateurs and allow the wet end of the cuttings to dry before inserting into a peat and sand mixture. A minimum temperature of 21°C (70°F) is needed and roots should be produced in about a month. New leaves should appear about two weeks after the roots; although quite small at first, they will quickly increase in size provided that the cuttings are not left too long in the mixture of peat and sand.

Over-grown rubber plants, which are too tall and spindly to be attractive, can be used to make two plants of more manageable size by the process of air layering. In this method of propagation, the top half of the plant is encouraged to produce roots of its own before it is actually severed from the main stem. Decide where you want the roots to form and then remove the closest leaf. Make a notch in the

Scindapsus aureus, or golden pothos, often needs pruning to keep it from growing leggy. Use the cuttings taken in spring or summer to form new plants.

35

To air layer a rubber plant, nick the stem and keep it open by inserting a pebble (1). Dust with rooting powder and wrap sphagnum moss around the area (2). Secure moss with clear polythene (3). Detach and pot up when roots have formed (4).

stem about 5cm (2in) in length and half the thickness of the stem. Hold the cut open by inserting a small pebble between the two sections of stem and dust the wound with rooting powder. Then wrap moist sphagnum moss around the entire area, securing it with clear polythene and soft twine. Signs of roots should be visible in about two months; when an ample number of them can be seen, remove the polythene and leave the moss ball intact. Cut the newly rooted plant from the mother plant just below the roots and insert it in a rich growing medium; maintain the temperature at 21°C (70°F) and keep the compost on the dry side until the plant has become established.

The parent plant will produce several new shoots from just below the cut and a bushier, well-furnished specimen should result. Unfortunately, the Swiss cheese plant (*Monstera deliciosa*), does not respond to air layering, and tends to remain ungainly looking when the top growth is removed. These plants are not easily propagated from cuttings, and almost all commercially grown plants are raised from seed sown in a high temperature.

Another form of layering involves placing plants with long strands of growth, such as *Ficus pumila*, near a boxful of potting mixture and directing the strands into the mixture, where they will root naturally. Once strong-growing roots have formed, the new plants can be severed from the parent and potted up.

Although African violet cuttings will root quite happily in water, a higher success rate will be achieved if the cuttings are inserted in a sand and peat mixture and kept at a constant temperature of 21°C (70°F). Select leaves which are firm, green and free from blemish and insert them gently into the rooting medium. Because the leaves are soft and furry, a very humid atmosphere may encourage leaf-rot; do not cover the cuttings with polythene or wet the leaves while watering the rooting medium. Each leaf will eventually produce a cluster of small plants around the base of its stalk and these can be detached and potted up, either teased apart and planted individually, or all in one pot. Although the plants may look bigger and better initially if planted in one pot, this practice usually results in less attractive mature plants, with flowers and leaves growing in all directions. Additionally, young plants should not be allowed to flower prematurely and as a rule the first flower buds should be removed as soon as they are seen.

Poinsettia cuttings are taken from new growth in early summer; 10cm (4in) sections are taken, cutting just below a leaf. Remove the bottom leaf and insert the cuttings as quickly as possible into pure peat. Despite the speed of the operation, they will still wilt alarmingly and will need frequent and regular spraying if they are to survive. Once they have made a reasonable amount of root the plants can be potted up into a rich mixture; when they have settled down, remove the growing tips to produce a bushier, more attractive plant.

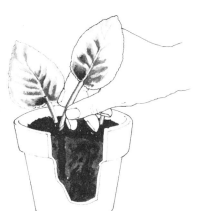

To propagate African violets,
select and detach strong,
healthy leaves from the plant.

Gently insert these into a
rooting medium kept at a
temperature of 21°C (70°F).

Once roots have formed, small
leaves will appear at the base.
Well-grown African violets (above).

37

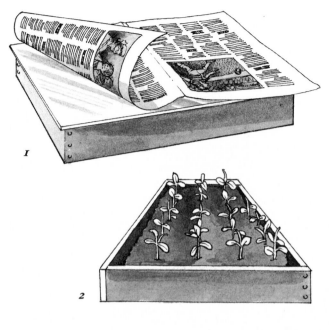

Sansevieria cuttings are slightly out-of-the-ordinary in that they are made from cutting the main stem into sections and pressing them, vertically, into boxes filled with pure peat. Once roots and leaves have formed, the original stem section is buried when the new plant is potted up.

Raising new plants from seed may seem less exciting than other methods of propagation, but it is certainly the most economical way of aquiring the greatest number of plants in the shortest possible time. Do not skimp on the cost of a packet of seed or the entire exercise may prove disappointing.

Use boxes or shallow pans filled with a peat and sand mixture; press down the compost gently — never ram it. Finally, moisten the surface with water from a watering can fitted with a fine rose and sow the seed.

Follow directions on the seed packet for the best results; after sowing, cover the box or pan with a plate of glass and then a sheet of newspaper. Lift and turn the glass regularly and once germination has occurred, remove the newspaper so the seedlings are exposed to light. Leave the seedlings to grow on until they are large enough to handle, then lift them by their leaves and transfer them, properly spaced out, into similar boxes or pots filled with a conventional potting mixture.

Given reasonable amounts of warmth, moisture and light, a very wide range of plants can be grown from seed, including such exotics as coffee and banana plants. Although it may take some time from sowing to the fully grown specimen and plenty of patience is required, many people find this method of plant propagation the most rewarding.

Propagation of ferns from spores is a similar operation to propagation of new plants from seeds. Fill a shallow clay pan with a mixture of equal parts (by volume) of peat and loam, with a little sharp sand added for drainage and a little charcoal to keep the

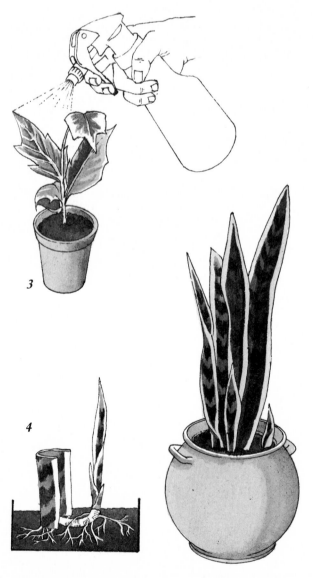

After sowing seeds, cover the pan with a sheet of glass and newspaper to keep the atmosphere moist and dark until germination has occurred (1). Then remove the paper to expose the young plants to sunlight; removing the glass gives them room to grow and reduces their vulnerability to damping off (2). Cuttings which have not yet rooted are liable to wilt and may need frequent and regular spraying to keep the leaves turgid. Poinsettia cuttings are a case in point (3). Sansevieria can be easily propagated from leaf cuttings inserted vertically in a sandy compost; tiny complete plants will grow from the newly-formed roots (4).
Opposite: a well-grown nephrolepis. Propagation is by division, by pegging down its creeping stems and severing the new young plant when rooted, or from spores collected from the undersides of the leaves.

compost sweet. To collect the spores, take a frond which has dark brown spore cases on its under side and put it in a paper bag. Shake the bag vigorously to release the spores, which will then collect at the bottom of the bag. Before sowing, firm the surface of the compost and moisten with water from a fine-rosed watering can. Once the spores have been sown, cover the pan with a plate of glass and put the pan in a larger container which has been partially filled with water. It is essential that the compost is never allowed to dry out; the pan should be of clay to allow the water to permeate. It should also be kept out of direct sunlight, but constant warmth must be maintained. From one to three months later, depending on the type of fern propagated, a

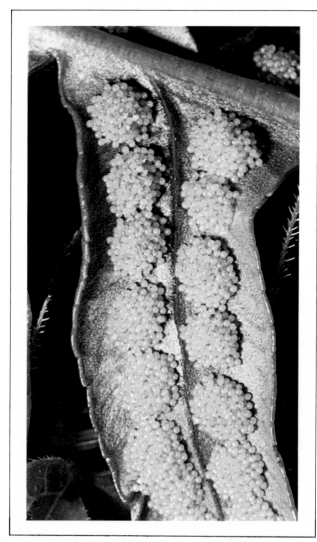

Underside of the hardy common fern, Polypodium vulgare, showing the clusters of ripe spores ready for dispersal.

moss-like growth will appear on the surface of the compost; this is the prothallus, an intermediary stage which will in turn produce tiny new ferns.

Once these ferns appear, remove the glass so they get plenty of fresh air. When they are large enough to handle, prick out groups of tiny ferns into pots filled with similar compost and put them in a shaded, airy place. When they have grown slightly larger, pot them up into individual containers.

Dealing with pests and diseases

The warm, moist growing conditions that make for first-class, healthy indoor plants are, unfortunately, perfect for innumerable pests and diseases which also thrive in warm moist environments. By far the best step in controlling such problems is a preventative one, that is, to avoid introducing them into the house. Although this may appear as an over-simplification, many a newly-bought plant has arrived home with the added bonus of greenfly, whitefly or mealybug. Before buying a plant, inspect it thoroughly for any signs of infection or infestation.

The most common problems you are likely to encounter are listed below, together with method of control. No matter what sort of pesticide or fungicide you use, keep in mind that results can be disastrous for the plant in question and also dangerous to the user, if instructions are not followed exactly. Always wear rubber gloves when handling pesticides. Plants should be taken into the protected area of a garage or shed where fumes will not blow about and the plant should not be exposed to strong sunlight immediately after spraying the foliage. It is also a good idea to leave the plant out of the house until all the unpleasant odours connected with spraying have disappeared. Often, a single application will not be sufficient and repeat applications should be made according to the manufacturer's instructions. When spraying, pay particular attention to the undersides of the leaves, where pests would otherwise be sheltered from the spray. Red spider mites and scale insects are notorious for preferring leaf undersides.

Aphids

These are also known as greenfly and blackfly depending on the colour of the species. They are small, plump and usually wingless pests, and are always found in large colonies. One or other species of aphids attack almost every cutltivated plant. Most species are foliage feeders but some attack the woody parts and others feed on the roots. When feeding they force their needle-like mouthparts into the plant sap stream and pump in digestive juices before sucking up the sap. The saliva is often toxic to the plant tissue and can cause severe discolouration of the leaves. The removal of the sap weakens the plant and the punctures can act as a point of entry for

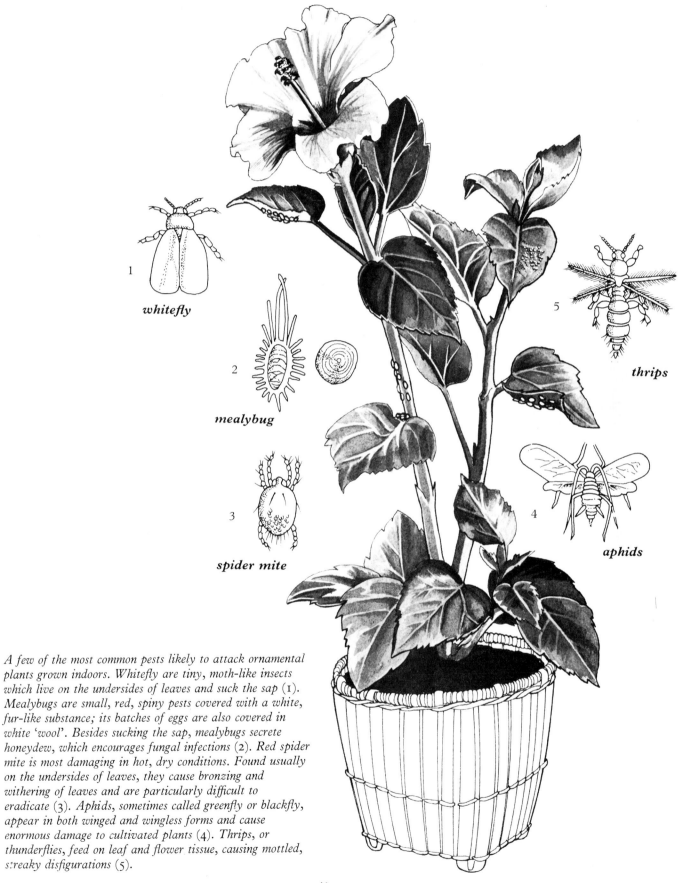

1
whitefly

2
mealybug

3
spider mite

5
thrips

4
aphids

A few of the most common pests likely to attack ornamental plants grown indoors. Whitefly are tiny, moth-like insects which live on the undersides of leaves and suck the sap (1). Mealybugs are small, red, spiny pests covered with a white, fur-like substance; its batches of eggs are also covered in white 'wool'. Besides sucking the sap, mealybugs secrete honeydew, which encourages fungal infections (2). Red spider mite is most damaging in hot, dry conditions. Found usually on the undersides of leaves, they cause bronzing and withering of leaves and are particularly difficult to eradicate (3). Aphids, sometimes called greenfly or blackfly, appear in both winged and wingless forms and cause enormous damage to cultivated plants (4). Thrips, or thunderflies, feed on leaf and flower tissue, causing mottled, streaky disfigurations (5).

41

fungal and bacterial diseases. Aphids are also major carriers of viral diseases. Finally, aphids disfigure plants by covering the surfaces with sticky honeydew which often becomes infected with sooty moulds.

The major problem with aphids is their enormous breeding rate. Fortunately, this is reduced by natural predators such as ladybird and lacewing, but even so, damaging infestations can build up very quickly. This emphasizes the need to watch for any sign of trouble.

Root aphids, which can be very damaging to cacti, succulents and many ornamental plants, are moved from one plant to another by ants which 'farm' them for their honeydew. Another specialized species is the woolly aphid which is covered with white waxy wool and feeds on branches and pruning cuts, causing unsightly gall-like growths.

Foliage-feeding aphids are easy to control, being susceptible to many systemic and non-systemic insecticides.

The control of woolly aphids presents rather more of a problem because of the protective waxy covering and it is therefore necessary to use a forceful spray of malathion, gamma-HCH or dimethoate.

Root aphids are the most difficult to deal with. Either lift the plants and then wash the roots free of aphids or apply soil drenches of malathion or pirimiphos-methyl.

Mealybugs

These pests look rather like woolly aphids because of their covering of powdery white wax. They are sap suckers, attacking the stems and leaves, and will generally be found around the buds and leaf joints. Some species feed on roots and are particulary common on cacti and succulents. Mealybugs are resistant to many pesticides although malathion and dimethoate are still effective. An added complication in controlling mealybugs is that cacti and succulents tend to be senstive to many chemical sprays. Tests should therefore be made on single plants or on a few leaves of each species to ensure that the spray has no adverse effects on the plant. Wiping the leaves with methylated spirits is another form of control, if rather cumbersome.

Whitefly

Adult whitefly are rather like tiny white moths with a covering of powdery wax on their bodies. They are usually found feeding on the undersides of the younger leaves and flutter about if disturbed. The females lay eggs on the undersides of the host plant's leaves. These hatch out into small, flattened oval green scale-like larvae which feed by sucking the plant sap. Eventually they turn into waxy pupae from which the new adults later emerge, the whole cycle taking 3-4 weeks.

The commonest species attacking ornamental plants is the greenhouse whitefly. During the summer this may also attack outdoor plants.

Until recently, whitefly were a particularly difficult to control because only the adults were susceptible to available insecticides. Consequently repeated treatments had to be given over a period of at least a month in order to deal with new generations of adults which emerged from the younger stages. Fortunately, some new insecticides, notably resmethrin, bioresmethrin and pirimiphos-methyl are active against the larval stage, though even these chemicals have no effect on the eggs and pupae. Still it is now possible to control whitefly effectively by using a programme of three sprays at 3- to 4-day intervals, directing the spray on to the undersides of the leaves where the insects are feeding. A solid bar containing insecticide can also be hung up indoors to control these pests.

Scale insects

Scale insects spend most of their lives firmly fixed to the plant surface where the adult females look rather like miniature limpets. The eggs of some species are protected by white waxy wool but in others they are simply retained within the scale of the female crawlers which move to a suitable feeding site and then settle down to suck the plant sap. They are common on many plants, indoor and outdoor, and are a particular nuisance in the greenhouse. All species produce sticky honeydew which becomes infected with sooty moulds.

Scale insects are difficult to control because both the eggs and the adults are protected by the tough scale. Spray treatments with dimethoate, malathion or pirimiphos-methyl may be used giving two or three applications at 14-day intervals. This treatment is best started when the eggs have hatched and the young crawlers are still on the move. If the infestation is not too heavy the adults can be scraped off or removed with cotton wool soaked in methylated spirits and wrapped around an orange stick.

Thrips

Thrips are minute, slender, dark-coloured insects. They feed on the underside of the leaves by scraping the surface and then sucking up the sap. Leaf damage shows up as a yellow or silvery mottling while infested flowers develop white streaks. Attacked plants become stunted and deformed. Thrips also transmit virus diseases. Both indoor and outdoor plants are subject to attack but this pest is more serious indoors where its breeding is encouraged by hot dry conditions and is continuous instead of being restricted to summer as it is outdoors. Thrips are fairly readily controlled by most insecticides. Treatment should be given at the first sign of attack and repeated at 7- to 10-day intervals as necessary.

Mites

Mites, including the well-known red spider mites, are extremely small creatures, being just visible to the naked eye as globular pinheads. They are not insects but are included as they are dealt with in a similar way. They are common and widespread sap-feeding pests, both indoors and out. Attacked foliage quickly develops a yellow speckling which later becomes bronzed. Some species produce silken webs which enable them to pass from one plant to another.

Mites are rather difficult to control as only a limited number of pesticides are effective against these pests. Malathion, dimethoate, resmethrin and biroresmethrin all give a degree of control. Even so, repeated applications at 7- to 10-day intervals are usually necessary because of the resistance of the eggs to most garden chemicals. Do not keep using the same insecticide as this will result in a quicker build-up of resistance. As mites thrive in dry, overcrowded conditions, keeping an adequately humid atmosphere around the plants will control the numbers indoors.

Botrytis

This fungal infection is a very common problem, both indoors and out. It is usually associated with cool, damp growing conditions and excessive moisture. Its common name, grey mould, is very descriptive of the main symptom: fluffy, grey growths on the leaves, stems and flowers of infected plants. Initially, the disease enters the plant through a wound or through dead or dying tissue and dead leaves or flowers left on a plant are particularly vulnerable. Because the spores of botrytis are always present in the air, poor growing conditions can quickly lead to a severe attack.

The best precaution is to ensure that plants are not overcrowded and that air can circulate freely. If a plant is slightly infected, remove and burn those parts of the plant showing symptoms. Improve the growing conditions by raising the temperature, both night and day, and giving more ventilation. Badly infected plants should be removed and destroyed, as it is unlikely they will recover.

Mildew

This is the name given to a type of plant disease which shows in the leaves, shoots and sometimes the flowers of infected plants as a surface covering of a powdery white or greyish fungus. Basically, there are two types of mildew. Powdery mildews are entirely superficial and grow on the surfaces of a plant as a white powdery coating; chains of spores are produced in the coating and these spores spread the infection.

The downy mildews grow deeply into the inner tissues and send up threads through the surface which produce infective summer spores; the spores are eventually released into the soil. Downy mildews are seen on the surface only as a greyish patch of furry growth but they are far more injurious than the superficial powdery mildews.

Plants which are grown in poorly ventilated, moist air conditions are particularly vulnerable and also plants which are too dry at the roots. At the first sign of mildew, remove and destroy the infected parts and spray the plant with a fungicide. It is equally essential to find the plant a more congenial growing position.

Before using a fungicide, make sure that it is chemically suitable for the particular plant. Proprietary sprays containing dinocap or zineb are most common, but chrysanthemums and begonias should be sprayed or dusted with a sulphur-based fungicide.

Virus

A virus is a minute particle, visible only under the electron microscope, which causes disorders or diseases in living cells. Yellow or brown spots, streak or ring patterns on the leaves may be an indication of virus. Other viral symptoms on the leaves are dark green areas along the veins, a loss of green colour in the veins or a complete yellowing of the leaf. Streaks may appear on stems of infected plants. On flowers, white flecks or streaks of an unexpected colour or distortion may indicate viral infection. Less distinct symptoms of viral infection are a general stunting and reduction of vigour.

Some viruses adhere to the mouth parts of insects feeding on infected plants and they are then carried to healthy plants. Others are absorbed into the digestive system of the insect and from there pass into the salivary glands where the virus multiplies. When feeding, the insect injects saliva containing virus particles into plants and will remain a disease carrier all its life.

Because insects are major transmitters of viral infections, the elimination of pests is the best preventive measure against the spread of viruses. Plants propagated from infected material will contain virus particles, so make sure your source of plants is reputable. Regular inspection of all plants is another good precaution; suspect plants should be destroyed, as once a plant is infected there is no known cure.

HOUSEPLANT SPECIALITIES

Although the same basic rules apply to the majority of houseplants, some 'specialities' such as bottle gardens or bonsai trees do require some distinctive treatment to succeed in the home.

Bottle gardens

When growing a large selection of indoor plants it is impossible to provide within the walls of one room conditions that will be ideal for them all; ivy, for example, prefers a cool and dry atmosphere while philodendrons like a warmer and moister environment. Similarly, many ferns require close, damp and warm conditions which are totally impossible to provide in an average room.

One way of overcoming this difficulty is to offer the more demanding plants an environment of their own, a mini-greenhouse within a room. The Victorian Wardian case was the first such indoor greenhouse and its modern counterpart is the bottle garden, although a wide variety of glass containers can be used to achieve the same effect. Very elaborate and expensive containers can be bought, made of panels of clear and stained glass and leading, but a tropical fish tank is just as effective, far less expensive and is actually much easier to plant and maintain than a conventional bottle garden. A fish tank merely needs the lid removed, while the narrow neck of bottle gardens makes access to the plants more difficult and requires an assortment of improvised tools attached to long canes to keep the plants well tended.

Whatever the container, it must be clean, both inside and out, and warm soapy water is best. The glass should be rinsed and allowed to dry thoroughly before the potting mixture is introduced to avoid compost sticking to the side of the container. If you are using a bottle or carboy, make sure the cardboard is removed from the lid; if left in, mildew or other fungus will be encouraged to grow. When the container is completely clean and dry, use a cardboard tube to put in a layer of washed gravel to provide for drainage. Follow this with a layer of charcoal lumps and finally a layer of moist and crumbly peat or potting compost. The soil can either be loam or peat-based but it must be sterilized to kill unwanted seeds and pests. In a closed environment, it is absolutely imperative that the plants themselves are healthy and pest free as these conditions form a perfect environment for most diseases.

The choice of plants for a bottle garden should be made with care. It is best to avoid flowering plants, such as African violets, as once the flowers have faded they must be removed from the container or fungal infection will quickly set in. It is not only important to use small plants at the outset, but also to know that they grow slowly. *Selaginella* is a case in point; this delicate fern-like foliage plant seems at first glance eminently suitable for the bottle garden. If given ideal surroundings, it will grow at a rapid pace and quickly smother neighboring plants. *Pilea* is another highly invasive plant well kept out of a bottle garden with mixed planting. However, both of these plants are attractive, and might be tried used on their own in large containers.

Among the most attractive foliage plants for colour are varieties of crotons (*Codiaeum reidii* and *Codiaeum holufiana*) begonias (*Begonia rex* and *Begonia maculata*) and starfish bromeliads (*Cryptanthus*). Variegated ivies such as *Hedera helix* 'glacier' are ideal for ground cover, as well as *Ficus pumila*. Chlorophytums, dracenas and aphelandras are ideal as larger plants to give height to the display. Among the intermediate-sized plants are peperomias (*Peperomia hederaefolia*, *P. magnoliaefolia*), and the distinctive leaf veins of fittonias (*F. argyroneura*, *F. verschaffeltii*) will add to the interest of the garden.

Among the ferns, there are many suitable subjects. The bird's nest fern (*Asplenium nidus*) is particularly attractive and the brake ferns (*Pteris*) can be had in a variety of sizes and variegations. The holly-leaf fern (*Cyrtomium falcatum*), with its glossy, dark-green, leaf-like fronds, is suitable for larger containers as it tends to be a robust grower and the maidenhair fern (*Adiantum capillus-veneris*) actually prefers being grown in a glass container.

Once you have selected the plants, you can begin assembling the garden. It is a good idea to plan the spacing of the plants beforehand on a piece of paper the same size as the area to be filled. Allow plenty of space for growth so no overcrowding occurs. Prepare the plants for insertion by gently removing most of the soil from around the roots. Work from the outside edges of the container towards the centre, using a spoon (attached to a bamboo cane if necessary) to make planting holes in the soil. Use a bamboo tweezer for small plants and a hooked wire for larger ones. Spread out the roots of each plant with a fork and then cover them with the soil. An empty wooden cotton reel attached to a bamboo stick can be used for tamping down the soil around each plant.

When the planting is complete, pour in enough water to moisten the growing medium, but not to saturate it. Replace the lid, and put the container in a slightly shaded, warm place. Condensation will probably form within a few days at the top of the bottle or tank; if none appears, add a little more water. If, on the other hand, there is so much condensation that the glass is obscured, remove the lid or stopper for a few days. Once a state of equilibrium has been reached, water the plants every few months and then only sparingly. Regular removal of all dead and dying leaves is an essential task, as fungal infections can rapidly reduce a bottle garden to an untidy mess of rotting foliage.

When filling a bottle garden, use a funnel and tube to keep the glass from becoming soiled by compost or grit.

After choosing suitable plants, gently insert them into the growing medium with a bamboo tweezer or hooked wire.

Water moderately after planting and replace the lid. Below: an imaginative grouping of bottle gardens.

Hanging baskets

It was not really practicable to grow plants in hanging baskets indoors before the advent of baskets with built in drip trays. Now, however, many plants that are best displayed in hanging baskets can be easily accommodated indoors. Baskets can be placed anywhere — on walls, hanging from rafters, in front of windows or above the centre of a doorway. Make sure when selecting a position that it is high enough not to be a hazard to the tall and yet low enough to be reached for watering and other maintenance. As a rule, baskets which are planted for seasonal display and hung outdoors should be tightly packed with a variety of plants, while those grown indoors on a more permanent basis should contain one species only, for ease of management, and be planted rather sparingly, to allow room for growth.

Hanging baskets come in a small range of sizes and are either round or semi-circular in shape. They are usually made of strong wire which is often plastic-coated or else entirely of a strong polythene. Other containers can be used, such as clay or terra cotta pots or oil cans, but the latter will need very thorough cleaning before planting. Also, drainage holes must be punched in the bottom to release excess water.

All containers must be hung from reliable supports strong unrusted chains or cables are best and rope should be avoided as it tends to stretch and rot. The fixing point for the complete basket should be a secure hook fitted into a sturdy base, such as a solid rafter, brick (not mortar) or onto a solid metal railing. If the basket is grown near a single light source, the hook should be able to be turned by a quarter daily so that all plants get equal exposure to light.

Before filling the basket, make sure it is resting on a firm base; a big flower pot or bucket is suitable. If the basket has open lattice sides, line it with sphagnum moss. Lay the moss in a thick even sward with no thin patches and do not attempt to cover more than the bottom third of the basket. Alternatively, use heavygrade black horticultural polythene. When using polythene, cut and tuck it neatly in around the top edge of the basket and make a few drainage holes in the base.

After the lining has been fixed, fill the basket by one third with good compost and firm it down gently, to avoid the completed level sinking dramatically after the first watering. Begin adding the plants; if plastic is used as a liner, cut slits in it large enough to insert the root ball. If using sphagnum, the plant stem should rest against the moss, while the roots are in contact with the soil. Place another layer of sphagnum around the sides of the basket and proceed to fill with compost so the basket is two-thirds full. Put in a second row of plants and fill the basket with the remaining compost so that it is filled nearly to the rim. Polythene-lined baskets can have a second row of slits made and a second layer of plants inserted in the same way as the first.

When planting a hanging basket, support it in a bucket; it is generally easier to fill and plant from the bottom up.

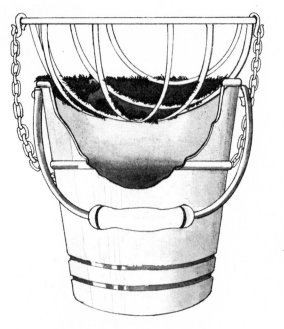

The completed basket should be well watered and allowed to settle for a couple of weeks before it is hung in its permanent position.

The type of plants grown depends very much on the amount of light available, but generally, those with a drooping or trailing habit of growth look best. In hot, sunny conditions, Christmas cactus is an excellent subject. For a less well lit spot choose from the many named varieties of ivy, philodendron or ferns.

The maintenance of hanging baskets is similar to that of pot-grown plants. Check regularly for water and give those plants which need a moist atmosphere a spray of tepid water now and again, even daily in hot dry weather. Feeding is not likely to be necessary immediately after planting; give liquid feed once the plants have settled down and are seen to be actively growing. Remove fading flowers to keep the basket attractive and also prevent energy wasted in seed formation. Remove dead and dying foliage as well, for visual reasons and also to discourage the advent of pests and diseases.

Bonsai

Although colourful packets labelled 'Bonsai seeds' are available from many garden centres and seed catalogues, this description is far more fanciful and hopeful than realistic. There is really no such thing as bonsai seed; what the packets contain is an assortment of tree seed which will produce ordinary seedlings. These can then be doctored by judicious training and pruning into bonsai trees, but it is no easy task. Many books have been written about the art of bonsai and mature specimens have changed hands for vast sums of money. Still, it is worth a try if you are intrigued by the science of controlling a tree's growth and form.

The cost of a seed packet should provide you with a reasonably interesting assortment but a quick walk through local woodlands or orchards is an equally good source. Besides the seeds themselves, young seedlings can sometimes be found growing which are dwarfed naturally or unusually shaped. Although conifers, such as pines, are excellent subjects for bonsai they are notoriously difficult to transplant. If you are attempting moving conifers take several to allow for some failures. If they are carefully lifted and potted up, an instant potential bonsai tree can be had, saving a year or two in time.

The word 'bonsai' literally means 'planted in a shallow vessel'; this practice restricts the growth of

Although they can be brought indoors for short periods of time for display, bonsai are essentially outdoor plants from the temperate zone. Without exposure to winter cold and summer heat, they would be unable to survive.

the plant and is combined with regular root and branch-pruning to keep the tree stunted. In classical bonsai, there are a number of highly formalised styles, with the trees trained into living sculptures. The young seedlings are shaped by means of wire spiralling round the stems and branches; supple wood is necessary at this stage to avoid breakage. The Japanese highly prized mature bonsai trees which were found growing naturally, perhaps in a rock cranny or very exposed position. Infinite care is needed to successfully lift and transplant such a mature tree, which probably adds to its value.

A word of warning about bonsai trees is necessary: they are most definitely not indoor plants. As one of the main requirements for a bonsai tree is that it is slow growing, species selected are almost invariably from a temperate climate. This means that they actually need exposure to the elements, the winter cold and the summer sun, to survive and they would quickly succumb to the warm, dry conditions indoors. Although a bonsai tree can be brought indoors for short periods of time, as a temporary decorative feature, it is essentially an outdoor plant.

Hydroponics

In recent years there has been a marked increase in the number of hydroponic growing kits available from florists and garden centres. Although many nurserymen have given their own trade names to hydroponic growing systems, they are actually all very similar. The first requirement is a watertight container of sufficient depth to accommodate the pot in which the plant is growing and enough inert clay granules for placing around the roots of the plant The granules are manufactured from treated clay and are very porous, absorbing about one-third of their own weight in water. Besides the container and the expanded granules, a water-level indicator is necessary to ensure that the correct water level is maintained and that there is never more than 7.5cm (3in) around the bottom of the pot. The container is filled to this maximum depth and is allowed to drop to the minimum mark on the indicator before refilling. It is essential that the indicator should remain at minimum for at least five days before refilling; this allows for the maximum amount of air to circulate around the roots of the plant. In cold weather, make sure you use tepid water and fill the container to the half-way, rather than the full mark.

The last factor is nutrient for the plant, as neither the water nor the clay particles provide any sort of food. A special fertilizer has been developed for hydroponic growing and it allows the plant to draw in as much nutrient as it requires. The problem of over-fertilizing the plant doesn't arise, although care

must be taken to recharge the unit when all the available nutrient has been absorbed. The time span will vary according to the size of the container but it is usually at six-month or yearly intervals. A hydroponic unit will have complete cultural instructions attached and if they are followed, you should have no trouble growing first-class healthy plants. One word of advice: if you are growing a group of plants in a large container with one indicator serving all the plants, it is essential that all the plant pots in the container are the same depth.

A cut-away section through a hydroponic container showing the inner container, expanded clay particles and indicator.

Tools and equipment

With ten or twenty house plants in pots around the house you do not need many tools. Any old spoon and fork can be used to loosen the surface of the soil, and a sharp knife will serve for all your cutting and pruning work. A bottle or two will be enough to keep your water for watering. However, you might still prefer to make use of some of the equipment especially designed for looking after house plants.

A watering can with a long spout, deep set in the can, is an important adjunct. This can be in plastic for lightness, or in galvanized iron or brass; the fine rose at the top of the spout reaches into window boxes and onto the gravel base of plant troughs. A plastic bucket is useful for moistening peat or peat compost. If you are in doubt about the amount of water needed, then buy a moisture meter, which comes with a handbook giving recommended readings. A hygrometer will give you the moisture content of the air, and a thermometer will check the temperature.

In order to give plants like ferns the daily shower they like, a spray or syringe can be used to direct a fine mist of water over the leaves. These are usually plastic and light. Should you need to use insecticides and pesticides, then do be careful to use a different spray. Hairy or furry-leaved plants which cannot be sprayed can be dusted with a small brush with soft bristles, and large leathery leaves can be wiped over with cotton-wool or a soft cloth dipped in tepid water. There is also a special spray designed for this purpose.

As well as keeping a sharp knife for removing offsets and cuttings and a pair of shears for pruning and taking stem cuttings, a sharp pair of scissors for dead-heading and cutting twine and string might be useful.

A small hand trowel and fork can be used for working in a window box, for filling pots with compost and for keeping the soil regularly aerated, but this can just as well be done with your old fork and spoon.

You will need compost, seed compost and bulb-fibre, unless you grow your plants hydroponically. Canes for supporting plants, green or natural in colour will be needed, and bass string or plastic ties for attaching them to the stems.

1 Max/min thermometer
2 Supporting rings
3 Hygrometer
4 Self-watering device
5 Moisture meter

6 Leaf shine
7 Liquid fertilizer
8 Thermostat
9 Atomizer
10 Twine

PICTURE CREDITS
A-Z Botanical Collection: endpapers
Amsterdam Bruys: 35
P. Ayres: 12
Steve Bicknell: 10, 22, 29, 30, 31, 35
Michael Boys: 19
Camera Press: 6/7

Paul Forrester: 39
Natural History Photographic Agency: 40
D. Smith: 26
H. Smith: 9, 47(B)
V & A Plantiques: 29